The Evolution of Government and Politics in

FRANCE

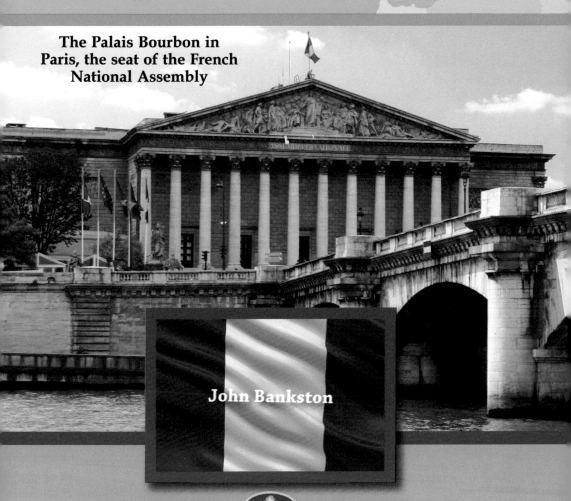

The Palais Bourbon in Paris, the seat of the French National Assembly

John Bankston

Mitchell Lane

PUBLISHERS

P.O. Box 196
Hockessin, DE 19707

Mitchell Lane
PUBLISHERS

The Evolution of Government and Politics in

CHINA
EGYPT
FRANCE
GERMANY
GREECE
IRAQ
ITALY
NORTH AND SOUTH KOREA
THE UNITED KINGDOM
VENEZUELA

PUBLISHER'S NOTE: The facts in this book have been thoroughly researched. Documentation of such research can be found on pages 44-45. While every possible effort has been made to ensure accuracy, the publisher will not assume liability for damages caused by inaccuracies in the data, and makes no warranty on the accuracy of the information contained herein.
The Internet sites referenced herein were active as of the publication date. Due to the fleeting nature of some web sites, we cannot guarantee that they will all be active when you are reading this book.

Printing 1   2   3   4   5   6   7   8   9

Library of Congress
Cataloging-in-Publication Data

Bankston, John, 1974–
 The evolution of government and politics in France / by John Bankston.
      pages cm — (The evolution of government and politics)
 Includes bibliographical references and index.
  ISBN 978-1-61228-583-2 (library bound)
 1. France—Politics and government—Juvenile literature. I. Title.
 JN2597.B24 2015
 320.944—dc23
                                             2014008882

eBook ISBN: 9781612286204

PBP

Contents

CHAPTER 1

Being French

Every 10 years, people across the United States are asked to fill out a form and mail it back to the government. The form asks how many people live in their home, how much money they make, their marital status, and many other questions. This form is part of the US Census. Conducting this count of households is a requirement found in the country's constitution.

Although originally designed to determine the number of representatives each state should have in Congress, the census today also asks respondents to identify themselves by race. Such a government-sponsored request could not exist in France. It would be illegal.

Many US citizens hyphenate. They might call themselves Italian-American, African-American, or Mexican-American. People who live in France call themselves French—regardless of where their parents, grandparents, or great-grandparents were born.

French citizens from a variety of ethnic and racial backgrounds ride this water taxi in the Port Vieux in Marseille.

Although the primary language of the United States is English, it is not an official language. Voting forms, driving tests, school lessons, and many other things have been translated into languages ranging from Armenian to Zulu. In France, French is the official language. Until quite recently, French children attending school were forbidden from speaking native dialects. Across a country the size of Texas, the pronunciation of words is expected to be identical. In Paris, the minister of culture works to keep English words like "e-book" and "hashtag" from being used.

Yet despite these efforts at uniformity, France remains one of the most welcoming countries on Earth. Only the United States and Canada have larger populations that were born elsewhere. All three nations are challenged with balancing an individual's desire for ethnic identity while at the same time preserving their country's national identity.

Those often-competing goals collided in France in 2004. That September, children were banned from wearing religious items like Christian crosses, Jewish yarmulkes, and Islamic headscarves to school.

France's population of Muslim immigrants is the largest in Western Europe. Many of them felt the bans were an attack on their religion. "It is unjust and I am very angry, angry yes, it's not just, it's a law, a segregation,"[1] said a Muslim woman.

Supporters of the new law, on the other hand, believed it was not about clothing or religion. It was about being French. One was Venus Kavoussian, who was born in Iran. "It's important that school stays non-political, non-religious," she said. "Personally I am living in France because it is a secular space,"[2] she said.

In the 1970s, radio commentator Eric Zemmour remembers that French Jews "took off their skullcaps as soon as they stepped into the street." They didn't want to offend anyone with their "expression of faith," he recalled on RTL Radio. Today, he continues, "the French way of living together" has been disrupted by groups that celebrate their ethnic or religious community over national identity. "Those who want to resist the steamroller are trapped, labeled racists or reactionaries."[3]

What it meant to be French was questioned after the country's revolution in 1789. France's new leaders wanted to transform

In 2011, women were banned from wearing full face veils in public in France.

Muslim schoolgirls protest 2004's prohibition against wearing headscarves to school. The sign on the right reads, "The headscarf is not contagious."

their ragtag country with its dozens of different ethnicities, languages, and values into a single nation sharing one language and one set of beliefs. Since then, the country has been led by kings and emperors, presidents and prime ministers. It has undergone so many changes that its current constitution is less than 60 years old. Despite having such a young government,

Worshippers pack a church. Catholics comprise 80 percent of the French population, while about 10 percent are Muslims.

France is dotted with Roman ruins such as this amphitheater in Arles, a town in southern France. Constructed around 90 CE, it served as an arena for chariot races.

France's history stretches back over two millennia. Many of the nation's roads, bridges and cities were developed by Roman conquerors.

CHAPTER 2
Taxes and Death

The barbarians were at the gates of Rome and the defenders couldn't stop them. In 390 BCE, the city of Rome was sacked by a group of invaders called the Gauls. Though the Romans were humiliated by the defeat, they learned a great deal about weapons and tactics. They put this knowledge to good use when they invaded southern Gaul in 125 BCE and annexed it. That was just for starters. Less than 70 years later, an army commanded by Roman statesman and military leader Julius Caesar defeated the last remaining tribe of Gauls.

Roman occupiers planted vineyards in southern Gaul and developed public baths, stadiums, and libraries. Roads were built. Cities like Paris and Lyon grew into urban areas with wide boulevards, sidewalks, and aqueducts providing indoor running water for the wealthy. Land was registered for tax collection. For centuries, Gaul was overseen by a strong central government with Roman administrators enforcing a code of laws across the country.

The Pont du Gard bridge was part of a Roman aqueduct that stretched for nearly 30 miles (50 km) from its source to the city of Nîmes. Aqueducts were among the most advanced water delivery systems in the ancient world.

For all of the success of the Roman Empire, by the fourth century CE a series of weak leaders and increasing debt made defending their far-flung territories impossible. In 410, a Germanic tribe known as the Visigoths sacked Rome. Seventy-six years later, the weakened Roman army was driven out of Gaul by another Germanic tribe, the Franks. The land they seized would be called France.

After seizing Gaul, the Franks controlled land where Belgium, Luxembourg, Switzerland, and France are today. By 800, when the Pope crowned the Frankish king Charlemagne as Holy Roman

Emperor, Gaul extended to the modern-day borders of Austria, Serbia, Germany, and Italy.

Charlemagne ruled millions of people from different backgrounds and beliefs. Provinces often had different laws and there was no common language. "It had not seemed particularly strange to most observers that subjects of the French king spoke Occitan, German, Basque, Breton, Catalan, Italian, Yiddish, or distinct French dialects, rather than standard French," explains historian David A. Bell. "Such diversity was the rule, not the exception, in most of Europe at the time."[1]

Charlemagne's grandsons fought amongst themselves, diminishing the monarchy's power. In 987, Frankish nobility elected a new ruler, Hugh Capet, who was the first in a direct

Hugh Capet captures Charles de Lorraine, one of his chief rivals, in 991. The victory helped Capet establish his authority. This illustration dates back to 1840.

line of 14 Capetian kings. During their rule, both the monarchs themselves and their subjects gained power. Although the king owned all of the land, he allowed the nobility to use it in exchange for their military support. The nobility in turn granted the land to farmers who worked it and knights who defended it. This system, called feudalism, began in France and spread across Europe.

In response to feudalism, skilled craftspeople and merchants formed guilds. By limiting membership and only allowing members to work in certain trades, competition was reduced. This increased the guild members' pay while maintaining quality. By organizing, they prevented excessive taxation by the nobility. Since they also held elections and often ran local governments, historians consider them an early example of European democracy.

In 1302, King Philip IV created the Estates-General. This "citizen's parliament" was a forum for the nation's "estates." Clergy made up the First Estate. The church owned huge tracts of land, but paid little in taxes. Many clergy were poor, but bishops were wealthy and powerful. They often gave advice to the king. The Second Estate was the nobles. They could hunt on peasant land and also did not pay taxes. In fact, the burden of paying taxes fell almost exclusively on the Third Estate. This, the largest group in France, included everyone from the poorest farmers to the richest merchants.

France was often at war. Regardless of outcome, these wars led to debt and increasing taxes to pay the debt. From 1337 to 1453, France fought against England after King Edward III's

Historian David F. Burg notes three major tax revolts from 1285 to 1314, and that "sixteenth century France experienced seemingly continual tax revolts. . . . During just the seventeenth century alone, in France there were fifty-eight uprisings against [sales taxes] and sixty-one against [customs duties]. France also experienced tax rebellions of major significance in the eighteenth century."[2]

In this fifteenth-century image, young clergymen receive their lessons. Educated, often wealthy and powerful, the clergy belonged to the First Estate. Their freedom from most taxes would incite a growing anger among the populace.

invasion. The long war was hugely expensive. In 1380, the Estates-General met to discuss ways to pay for it. Most of their discussion focused on raising taxes. When word of their plans got out, riots broke out across the country in protest. The poorest subjects struggled to survive. Higher taxes made their lives even more difficult.

Over 400 years later, these same conflicts over higher taxes and growing debt would topple the monarchy. A new form of government would beformed, followed by the gruesome public executions of the king and queen.

French nobles enjoyed sports such as hawking while the peasants (shown in the background) did all the work.

By the 13th century, the Parlement of Paris had developed into the country's central law court. Because jurists deciding its cases were handpicked, the Parlement was accused of favoritism.

CHAPTER 3
Jacobins, Emperors, and Kings

By the late 18th century, France was home to 26 million people—almost three times as many as its longtime rival England. It was also a nation in trouble.

In the late 1600s, under the reign of Louis XIV, France had fought expensive wars with the Netherlands, Spain, and England. The king also built the enormous Palace of Versailles. It drained the royal treasury while providing the perfect symbol of royal excess. Louis, who was also known as the "Sun King," justified these moves by claiming divine right. This was the belief that he and other monarchs received their powers directly from God.

After the French and Indian Wars ended in 1763, France lost much of its North American territory to the British. During the Revolutionary War, France provided desperately needed military and financial assistance to the American colonies in their struggle against the British. By the time the conflict ended in 1783, France was broke. The poor were starving. The monarchy was spending more money than it was taking in.

Construction of the Palace of Versailles began in 1664 during the reign of King Louis XIV and was completed 46 years later. The "Sun King" planned it as a monument to his own power, but to the poor it was a potent symbol of excess while France was slowly going broke.

In 1789, King Louis XVI called a meeting of the Estates-General—the first one since 1614. Unwilling to reduce his government's spending, the king hoped the gathering would support a tax increase. On May 5th, members of the First, Second and Third Estates entered the lush grounds of Versailles.

After nobles blocked the Third Estate's efforts to extract taxes from them, France's most-taxed group had had enough. On June 17th, they formed the National Assembly. They called upon members of the other two estates to join them in demanding fairer taxation and a greater voice in decision making.

Before Johannes Gutenberg's invention of moveable type and the printing press in the 1440s, books were assembled by hand. Only clergy and the rich owned them. The printing press reduced the cost of books—and more people could afford them. During the 1700s, even France's poor began to read and write. As they became better educated, many demanded more control of their lives.

The king was worried. He ordered his Royal Guard to block Assembly members from entering a meeting hall. Undeterred, they convened inside a nearby covered tennis court, where they quickly developed a new constitution.

The unrest soon turned to violence. On July 14, thousands of Parisians swarmed into Les Invalides, a home for wounded and disabled soldiers. The mob left with 10 cannons and thousands of muskets that had been stored in the basement, but very little ammunition. Their next target was the infamous Bastille prison, which contained large quantities of ammunition.

Despite the fortress's formidable defenses, it was poorly guarded. The structure was quickly overrun, its warden killed. His death was the first of many. The king's advisors warned him that the army could not protect him. Soldiers were unhappy with inadequate pay and the job's dangerous demands. They blamed the king. They wouldn't sacrifice their lives for his protection.

On August 26, 1789 the National Assembly approved its "Declaration of the Rights of Man." "Men are born and remain free and equal in rights,"[1] the first of its 17 articles began. The second concluded by explaining that the aim of political associations like the National Assembly was to preserve the "rights of man," which are "liberty, property, security, and resistance to oppression."[2]

It quickly became apparent that Louis wouldn't recognize the new document. The people were furious. On October 5th, a mob descended upon the Palace of Versailles. The loyal Swiss Guard was slaughtered. The king and his family, including his Austrian-born wife Marie Antoinette, abandoned Versailles for the smaller Tuileries Palace in Paris.

Within the newly formed National Constituent Assembly, members debated. Moderate leaders like Comte de Mirabeau favored holding elections while still having a monarch—similar to modern-day England. Others, like the Jacobins under the leadership of journalist Jean-Paul Marat and lawyer Maximilien Robespierre, thought this was unworkable. They were extremists who wanted to eliminate the monarchy and change French

The storming of the Bastille on July 14, 1789, is celebrated today as the opening blow in the French Revolution. Every year the French celebrate July 14 as Bastille Day, a national holiday.

The Jacobins took their name from the St. Jacobin monastery in Paris, where its members met to plan their strategy.

thought through aggressive reeducation and a new moral code emphasizing reason over religion.

In Versailles, Louis XVI had been sheltered. Paris was the center of the storm. He was not the only worried European monarch. Across the continent, royals and nobles had viewed the American Revolution with concern. The French Revolution was even more worrisome. The American colonies were 3,000 miles away. France was in their backyard.

The Austrian emperor promised to protect Louis XVI. In June 1791, the king slipped away from the palace. He was accompanied by his wife, his children, and a few loyal servants. The royal family was disguised, pretending to be servants of their son's governess. The ruse failed. They were captured at Varennes, less than 50 miles from safety. The escape attempt sealed the king's fate.

On April 20, 1792, France declared war against Austria. At first, France fared poorly. Austrian forces almost reached Paris. This threat of invasion, along with the king's perceived treason, increased the support for the Jacobins. Robespierre championed laws that allowed the new government to seize land owned by members of the Second Estate who fled the country. Land belonging to the clergy was also taxed.

The Jacobins began reeducating the French by requiring children to attend school. Government began providing more help for the poor. The guilds were outlawed.

On August 10, 1792, the king and his family were forcibly removed from Tuileries Palace and imprisoned. The following month, French leaders established what would become known as the First Republic. The king's reign was over. Soon his life would be too.

On January 21, 1793, 20,000 spectators, along with 1,200 members of the National Guard, crowded around the guillotine in the center of Paris. The soldiers surrounded the man they now called Louis Capet, preventing his escape and any attempts to save him. Louis was calm. He ascended the platform unaided. He proclaimed his innocence before being placed face down, his neck secured by a stock. At a signal the blade was released. A moment later, the king's head tumbled into a basket. The executioner held it aloft. At his feet, the royal blood dripped onto the ground below.

The king's execution was followed nine months later by his wife's. Louis XVI and Marie Antoinette were the most famous victims of the guillotine. They were not the last.

Robespierre acted like a dictator, unwilling to consider different opinions as he helped pass laws restricting his people's rights. The ideals of "liberty" and "equality" were weakened by rules ending the right to a public trial or an attorney.

Today the period of Jacobin rule is called "The Terror." More than 20,000 people were executed. Many were nobles or clergy accused of preferring a king—the Ancien Régime—to the new

Marie Antoinette being taken to her execution.

leaders. Many innocent peasants also died. A word from an unhappy neighbor or co-worker against them was enough for an arrest. Bearing a warrant from the Committee of Public Safety, armed men dragged the accused from their homes. Their trials were brief, their death sentences almost certain. Like the Salem witch trials in Massachusetts Colony 100 years earlier, mere accusations were considered evidence.

As the death toll grew, so did the opposition. On July 26, 1794 a debate within the National Convention turned against Robespierre. The outcry spread to the streets. The next day, his support was gone. The Convention voted to arrest Robespierre and his loyalists. Twenty-four hours later, he died like many of his victims—with his neck severed by the guillotine's blade.

After the Jacobins' downfall, a new bicameral legislature headed by a five-man group called the Directory gained power. Their strength came both from political organization and military victories. For years, eager volunteers had joined the French army. They wanted to preserve the new republic.

By 1799, however, the Directory had become unpopular, due in part to several military defeats. A dynamic young general named Napoleon Bonaparte led a coup that overthrew the Directory and established a new government called the Consulate. Originally it consisted of Napoleon and two other men. Napoleon quickly named himself First Consul. In 1802, he was elected First Consul for Life in a national vote. Two years later he became the nation's emperor.

He enjoyed widespread public support during his ascent. He not only ended the turmoil that had plagued the country for several years but also oversaw a rise in the overall standard of living. Under Napoleon, Roman Catholicism was reestablished as

Napoleon Bonaparte is often referred to by his first name. This is because he became France's emperor, and like its prior rulers no longer used his last name.

French artist Jacques-Louis David painted "The Coronation of Napoleon" in 1807. It measures 32 feet (9.8 m) by 20 feet (6 m). During the ceremony, Napoleon crowned himself to demonstrate his power.

the majority religion of France. In 1804, he organized the system of justice which bears his name. The Napoleonic Code eliminated the awarding of privileges to nobility. Today it remains as the basis for the French legal system. It is also utilized across South America and in Louisiana.

The general led his forces to battle across Europe during the Napoleonic Wars. By 1805, much of continental Europe was under French control.

In June 1812, Napoleon invaded Russia and penetrated as far as Moscow, the nation's capital. But as winter approached, he had to retreat. The country's poor roads, icy weather, and the French army's meager supplies did the rest. Napoleon had left France commanding over 500,000 men to begin the invasion. When he returned that December, less than 100,000 remained.

The emperor's failure led to the end of his reign in 1814. He was exiled to Elba, an island off the coast of Italy. Although he briefly returned to power, Napoleon officially abdicated on June 22, 1815. This time he was exiled to the remote island of St. Helena in the middle of the Atlantic Ocean.

Napoleon's departure left a leadership vacuum. The younger brother of Louis XVI stepped up to fill it and became Louis XVIII. The new king allowed the French to enjoy most of the same freedoms they'd had when the country was a republic. France's next ruler, King Charles X—another brother of Louis XVI—returned power to the clergy. During his reign he censored books and newspapers, strictly controlling what the French could read.

The Revolution of 1830 removed Charles X from the throne. He was replaced by King Louis-Philippe, a constitutional monarch who shared power with elected leaders. Despite the change, the new king ruled much like his predecessor. In 1848, another revolution brought expanded voting rights for the French.

The latest revolutionaries were socialists. They believed the 1789 Revolution's ideals had been lost. They also wanted all the French people to share in the nation's increasing wealth. These beliefs were rejected when voters abandoned the socialists. In the nation's first direct presidential election, Napoleon Bonaparte's nephew Louis-Napoleon overwhelmed four other candidates and drew nearly 75 percent of the votes.

The constitution for what became known as the Second Republic was the most democratic in Europe. Unfortunately, Louis-Napoleon's government grew restrictive. He felt hampered by a provision in the constitution preventing him from seeking re-election. So he arranged for a coup in 1851 that led to a new constitution allowing him to remain in power. French voters again gave him their support, with 92 percent favoring him. The following year, he declared himself as emperor.

Louis XVI's son—who would have succeeded him as Louis XVII if the revolution hadn't occurred—died in prison when he was just 10 and never ruled. When King Louis XVIII was crowned in 1814, he took the number "18" as a way to honor the executed king's son.

Ruling over what became known as the Second Empire as Napoleon III, he expanded the freedom of the press. He championed measures improving the lives of workers. But the Second Empire was destined to be short-lived. The neighboring German state of Prussia tricked him into declaring war in 1870. The Prussians quickly and decisively defeated the French. As part of the surrender terms, France had to give up the regions of Alsace and Lorraine along its border with the newly unified country of Germany.

Napoleon III stepped down. This marked the beginning of the nation's Third Republic, with free elections of all leaders. France recovered from the war. Its economy improved as the nation became a world leader in science and technology. New laws passed in the 1880s made education free. Not only would schools be state-run, for the first time they would also admit girls. There was a particular emphasis on requiring children to learn the country's language. As 19th century educational leader Ferdinand Buisson explained, "Teaching French, our beautiful and noble mother tongue, is the chief work of the elementary school—a labor of patriotic character."[3]

Soon France would need to demonstrate its "patriotic character." The battles fought by the French in the 20th century would not be waged at the ballot box or through street protests. Instead, they would be fought in the trenches with machine guns, grenades, and massive cannons.

Paris's Eiffel Tower was built to honor the 100th anniversary of the French Revolution.

CHAPTER 4

The World at War

The first time assassins tried to kill Archduke Franz Ferdinand, they failed. On June 28, 1914, Ferdinand was riding in a motorcade in Sarajevo, the capital of Bosnia-Herzegovina. A terrorist threw a bomb at his car, but it bounced off the convertible's folded roof before exploding. Ferdinand was unharmed but several others were injured in the blast. Ferdinand was being driven to the hospital to see those men when the second attempt occurred. This one succeeded.

Stepping from the crowd, Serbian nationalist Gavrilo Princip drew a pistol as Ferdinand's car approached the café where he was sitting. The driver, unfamiliar with the route, had stopped momentarily. Princip later said, "Where I aimed I do not know . . . I even turned my head as I shot."[1]

One shot killed Ferdinand, the other killed his wife. The deaths began one of the worst conflicts in human history, one that would leave millions dead.

Ferdinand was the heir to the throne of the empire of Austria-Hungary, which included both

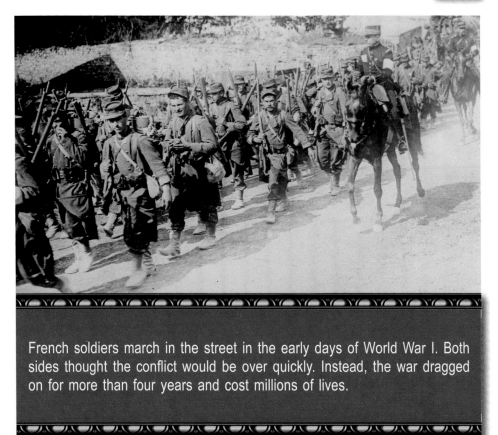

French soldiers march in the street in the early days of World War I. Both sides thought the conflict would be over quickly. Instead, the war dragged on for more than four years and cost millions of lives.

Bosnia-Herzegovina and Serbia. After the assassination, Austria-Hungary threatened to attack Serbia in retaliation for Princip's actions. Germany quickly offered its support to Austria-Hungary. Russia vowed to defend Serbia. France and England joined Russia. What became known as World War I quickly spread across much of Europe, eventually drawing in the United States.

Much of the war was waged on French soil, with a tremendous loss of life. Between 1914 and 1918, France lost more than a million and a half people, most of them young men serving in the military.

In 1919, the war ended officially with the Treaty of Versailles. It required Germany to return Alsace and Lorraine, the regions that it had taken in 1870, to France. Germany also had to pay a huge amount of money for the damage caused by the war. The result was considerable hardship in Germany and widespread resentment over the terms of the Treaty.

Over the next decade, France rebuilt while Germany continued to suffer. Following the 1929 US stock market crash, much of the world slipped into a depression. Like the US, the French government responded by enacting workplace reforms and attempting to increase employment. French workers were limited to a 40-hour workweek (today it is 35). Employers were also required to give their employees paid vacations.

The Hall of Mirrors in the Palace of Versailles was the scene of the signing of the 1919 treaty that officially ended World War I. The treaty required Germany to pay back enormous amounts of money—crippling the country economically while angering the people and helping to lay the foundation for World War II 20 years later.

France spent much of the 1930s focused on domestic matters. Government spending for social services increased, leaving less money available for the military. Tanks, planes, and ships grew obsolete.

French military spending focused on defense. Named after the country's Minister of War, the Maginot Line stretched along the border with Germany. Thousands of concrete structures and other obstacles formed a wall of defense, centered on large forts or "ouvrages." Each one bristled with heavy artillery and was manned by more than a thousand soldiers. The line appeared unbreakable.

In 1933, Adolf Hitler and his Nazi party rose to power in Germany. They gained popular support by promising that the country's suffering was over and her best days were on the horizon. The country stopped paying its war debts, pouring funds instead into the military. By the time Germany invaded Poland in 1939, it boasted a highly trained, motivated army operating some of the most advanced equipment of the era.

Germany invaded France in May the following year. The Maginot Line's designers had assumed that the Ardennes Forest (which lay north of the line) was impenetrable. They were wrong. Over one million Nazi soldiers, along with thousands of tanks and heavy field guns, cut a path through the dense woods. They also leveled the Line's northern edge and overwhelmed French defenses in the rest of the country.

In six weeks, the Germans had done what they were unable to do in four years during World War I: Force the French to surrender. Under the terms of the armistice, France ceded control of the north (including Alsace and Lorraine) to Germany. The rest of the nation was governed from a small resort town named Vichy.

The Vichy government was not independent. It followed Germany's orders and coordinated with them. Acting on its own, however, the Vichy government restricted the rights of French Jews. By the end of the war, some 70,000 would be deported to Nazi concentration camps, where most of them died. A once-

Standing between architect Albert Speer (left) and artist Arno Breker, Nazi leader Adolf Hitler visits Paris in June 1940, soon after his armies overwhelmed French resistance.

thriving Jewish community was decimated. Less than 2,500 of those deported ever returned.

Not everyone supported the new leaders. For years before the war, French General Charles de Gaulle had insisted that the defensive system centered on the Maginot Line would fail under an onslaught of German tanks. He was right. Instead of joining his superior, Marshal Pétain, as he formed the Vichy government, de Gaulle escaped to England. From there, he led 200,000 resistance fighters who used sabotage, snipers, bombs, and other means to wear down the occupiers within France. Meanwhile, he oversaw forces that won back some French colonies.

During his exile, the new French government sentenced de Gaulle to death for treason. His relationship with Allied governments was hardly better. US President Franklin Roosevelt at first preferred the Vichy leaders over de Gaulle, confiding to his son Elliott that "There is no man in whom I have less confidence."[2]

During World War I, de Gaulle was wounded five times in battle and spent more than two years as a prisoner of war.

Despite the challenges, de Gaulle believed that he and his Free French movement represented the best interests of his country. As for those who sentenced him to death, he said after the 1940 verdict, "They and I will have it out after the victory . . . We are France."[3]

In June 1944, thousands of American, British, and Canadian troops landed on the French beaches in Normandy. When they liberated Paris two months later, de Gaulle was made the chairman of the nation's provisional government.

After the war's end in 1945, the country faced enormous challenges. Roads, bridges, homes, and factories had been

Tens of thousands of Allied troops landed on Normandy beaches on D-Day, June 6, 1944. Omaha Beach, shown here, was the scene of the bloodiest combat. Many troops were cut down before they even left their assault boats.

destroyed. Rebuilding and assisting the millions of poor became a priority. The United States contributed funds for rebuilding. Just a year later, France faced a new challenge.

For more than a century, France had maintained colonies in Africa and other parts of the world. During World War II, France and other European countries benefitted from their colonies' resources. After the war, colonists wondered why—since they had helped their ruling countries remain free from Nazi control— couldn't they pursue independence as well? In France, colonial disputes threatened the nation's latest effort to become a republic.

In 1946, de Gaulle resigned from the presidency. He felt that the National Assembly had taken too much power. The Fourth Republic began in 1946 under President Felix Goulin, a socialist. Although Goulin and the National Assembly made concessions, they refused to grant independence to colonies such as Indochina. Talks with the Southeast Asian colony broke down the year Goulin took office. Under rebel leader Ho Chi Minh, the colony's desire for independence led to an eight-year war that resulted in a French defeat in 1954. Indochina formed the separate countries of Vietnam, Laos, and Cambodia. Less than a decade later, the United States would become embroiled in a similar, failing conflict in the region.

Not long after Indochina gained its independence, Algeria revolted against French rule. Even though it was located in North Africa, across the Mediterranean Sea, France regarded Algeria as part of its territory rather than a colony. The government sent 500,000 soldiers to crush the rebellion. Many French officers and conservatives felt the effort was insufficient. They planned a coup—hoping to end the Fourth Republic, install military rule, and retain Algeria.

With an area of 919,595 square miles (2,381,741 sq km), Algeria is the largest country in Africa and tenth-largest in the world.

With socialists and conservatives unable to compromise, France faced a civil war. On May 13, 1958, rebellious French military officers seized control of Algeria. On June 1st, the National Assembly granted Charles de Gaulle extraordinary powers to end the conflict and unify the nation. He wrote a new constitution, which created the Fifth Republic. The presidency would have new powers. De Gaulle hoped to maintain the country's independence from outside influence, especially from the United States.

Although French officers in Algiers attempted another coup in 1961, de Gaulle organized a settlement. After it was approved by French voters, Algeria gained independence while almost one million Algerians were allowed to immigrate to France. The next year, de Gaulle was re-elected by a landslide and repeated that triumph in 1965. Throughout his time in office, he focused on modernizing his country. The country became both an economic power and a military power.

From resistance fighter sentenced to death during World War II to France's president and author of her current constitution, Charles de Gaulle is one of the nation's most revered leaders.

The de Gaulle presidency and the nation faced its greatest test since Algeria in 1968. What began as a protest over tuition increases in Paris spread to include workers and students across the country. Strikes shut down industry and universities. Demanding greater reforms including a more democratic school system, the protesters seemed prepared to take down the Fifth Republic. Instead of caving, de Gaulle called for votes in the National Assembly. He managed to break the protests, and in the aftermath wages and working conditions improved while college education became more affordable and open.

DeGaulle stepped down in 1969. The Fifth Republic remains as the government of France.

What began as a student protest over tuition hikes in Paris almost grew into nationwide civil war. During a May 24, 1968, broadcast President de Gaulle asked for dictatorial powers. Here demonstrators listen to the request, which would soon be denied.

This aerial photograph of the Avenue des Champs-Élysées shows the thousands of demonstrators who answered de Gaulle's call for support on May 30, 1968. The president dissolved the National Assembly and called for new elections.

CHAPTER 5

Vive la Différence (Long Live the Difference)

Wars between France and Germany have cost millions of lives. After World War II, leaders from both nations hoped a partnership would eliminate future conflicts. In 1957, they joined four other countries to establish the European Economic Community. Now known as the European Union and boasting 28 members, it was designed to do more than just promote tariff-free trade among its members.

"The reconciliation and alliance of our two nations remained the essential guarantee of lasting peace on the continent,"[1] former French president Jacques Chirac explained in his autobiography. It was also hoped that by aligning the two countries economically, Germany and France would not go to war in the future. As a result of the alliance, the French no longer worry about wars with Germany.

Yet a nation so willing to challenge its own government would not be easily controlled by outsiders. In 2005, French voters rejected the proposed European Union constitution, concerned in part that allowing poorer countries to join the EU would bring more competition for jobs in France.

Today the French government resembles the US government in numerous ways. Both countries elect a president, who heads the executive branch. The two countries have bicameral, or two-house, legislatures. Both have a judicial system with several types of courts.

The French executive branch differs radically from the U.S. in one respect. In France, the president shares power with a prime minister. The president selects the prime minister, who is usually a member of the majority party in the National Assembly. It is as if Barack Obama and George W. Bush headed the US government at the same time!

The prime minister recommends people for the Council of Ministers, and the president appoints them. The president can call elections while the prime minister can be fired by the National Assembly.

In France, the National Assembly has 577 seats and proposes most of the laws. It makes the final decision if the 348-member

The National Assembly has 577 members representing a number of political parties who meet here and discuss proposed laws.

Senate disagrees. In the US, both the House of Representatives and the Senate must agree in order for a bill to be sent to the President, who vetoes it or signs it into law.

Until the early 1900s, members of the US Senate were selected by representatives of the people rather than by a direct vote by the people themselves. French senators are still elected that way. National Assembly members are elected by popular vote for five-year terms.

Perhaps the biggest difference between the politics of France and the politics of the United States lies in the number of political parties. Although there are numerous small parties in the US—such as the Green, Libertarian, and Socialist Parties—for more than 160 years the president has been a member of one of two main ones. While third-party candidates may earn enough votes to alter elections, the winners have always been either Democrats or Republicans. Virtually all members of Congress belong to one of the two main parties.

The Medici Palace, where the French Senate meets, in the Luxembourg Gardens, Paris.

In France, members of the National Assembly belong to a number of different parties. However, in recent years two major parties have dominated French politics. The Union for a Popular Movement (UMP) is a center-right party, which means it tends to support more conservative ideals. Under UMP leadership, France has sold state-run businesses like airlines and banks, although it still runs railways and the post office. Taxes have been lowered, while regulations and social services have been reduced.

The other major party in France today is the French Socialist Party (FSP). FSP promotes higher taxes on businesses and wealthier individuals, with the money used to provide more services to the poor and middle class. In 2012, the most recent voting, the current president and member of UMP Nicolas Sarkozy lost his reelection. Voters chose François Hollande, a member of the FSP, to replace him.

Hollande's election occurred in the aftermath of 2008's global recession. Since then, France has battled high unemployment and low growth. Hollande's message that Sarkozy's beliefs were similar to the ones that caused the recession resonated with voters. Hollande's move to increase taxes on higher earners, with a top rate of 75 percent, prompted a number of wealthy individuals and corporations to contemplate leaving France and relocating to countries with lower tax rates.

The French judicial system differs somewhat from the United States. Just as the US has civil and criminal courts, in France cases are heard in either the Judicial or Administrative Courts. Judicial Courts handle both civil and criminal cases involving individuals, while Administrative Courts focus on businesses. But France has nothing like the US Supreme Court, which can overturn laws it considers to be unconstitutional.

Launched in 1999, the euro has been adopted as the common currency of 18 European Union countries. In 2014, the euro was worth about $1.35.

Despite considerable turbulence in its past, France today is one of the world's most stable democracies. "France is strong and respected when it promotes its values, its heritage, its creativity," says French Minister of Culture Aurélie Filipetti. "Culture is one of our greatest strengths; it represents our heritage and a part of our future."[2] The strength of French culture and its political institutions will help guide the nation as it encounters the challenges of the 21st century.

François Hollande (center) campaigning in Narbonne, France, in April 2012. He wins the French presidential election on May 6, 2012.

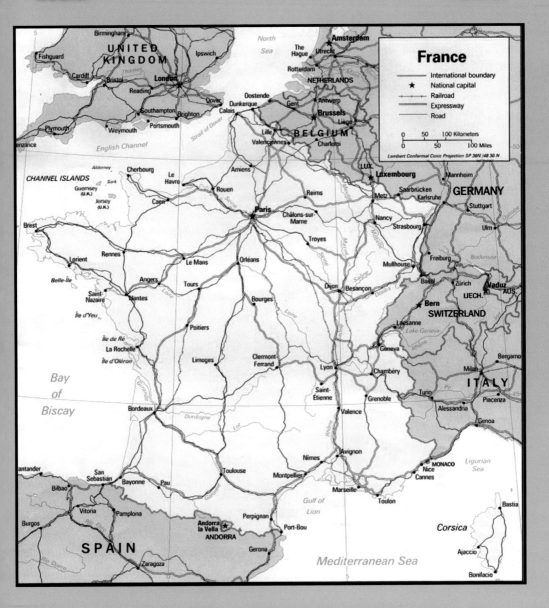

486   Frankish warlord Clovis seizes control of Gaul, an area which includes modern France along with Belgium, Luxembourg and Switzerland.

800   The Pope crowns the Frankish king Charlemagne as Holy Roman Emperor.

987   Frankish nobility elect Hugh Capet as king.

1200s   The Parlement of Paris, first organized during the reign of Philip Augustus (1180–1223), becomes the central law court under Philip's grandson, Louis IX ("Saint Louis").

1302   The first assembly of the Estates-General is called by King Philip IV.

1337   The Hundred Years War begins after English king Edward III's invasion of France and lasts until 1453.

1380   The Estates-General meets to discuss raising taxes to pay for the Hundred Years War, prompting riots to break out across France.

1422   Following the death of France's King Charles VI, the governors of Paris support a British claimant to the French throne.

1429   Charles VII's quest to become the next ruler of France is supported by teenage farm girl Joan of Arc; her leadership turns the tide of the war.

1431   Joan of Arc is burned to death at the stake.

1515   Newly crowned King Francis I becomes a strong supporter of education and the arts, laying the foundation for modern-day government support.

1648   The Parlement of Paris refuses to pass the monarch's tax increases; civil war erupts in Paris.

1685   King Louis XIV revokes religious freedoms granted by his grandfather; declaring himself "the Sun King," he rejects all other authority but God's.

1763   Defeat in the French and Indian War costs France much of its North American territory.

1789   A mob storms the Bastille.

1792   France establishes the First Republic.

1799   Napoleon Bonaparte leads a coup that overthrows the Directory and installs the Consulate.

1804   As the first emperor of the French Empire, Napoleon Bonaparte begins conquering most of Europe.

1815   After Napoleon is defeated at the Battle of Waterloo, the monarchy is reestablished.

1848   Napoleon's nephew Louis-Napoleon is proclaimed President of the Second Republic; it ends three years later with the establishment of the Second Empire.

1871   French defeat in the Franco-Prussian War marks the Second Empire's end and establishment of the Third Republic.

1914   France's participation in World War I costs about a million and a half lives.

TIMELINE

1919 The Treaty of Versailles requires Germany to pay enormous reparations to France and other countries harmed in the war.

1940 German forces defeat France during World War II; General Charles de Gaulle oversees a government-in-exile in London.

1944 Allied forces land in Normandy, France and soon liberate the country; de Gaulle sets up a provisional government in Paris.

1946 De Gaulle resigns and is replaced by Felix Goulin as the Fourth Republic begins.

1958 The Fifth Republic begins as De Gaulle returns to the presidency.

1981 François Mitterrand, a socialist, is elected president.

1995 Jacques Chirac is elected president, ending 14 years of Socialist presidency.

2005 Voters reject a proposed EU constitution.

2012 François Hollande, a socialist, wins the presidential election.

2014 Anne Hidalgo becomes first-ever female mayor of Paris.

CHAPTER NOTES

Chapter 1. Being French

1. Caroline Wyatt, "French headscarf ban opens rifts." BBC, February 11, 2004. http://news.bbc.co.uk/2/hi/3478895.stm

2. Ibid.

3. Georg Lentze, "Islamic headscarf debate rekindled in France." BBC News, April 2, 2013. http://www.bbc.co.uk/news/world-europe-21997089

Chapter 2. Taxes and Death

1. David Avrom Bell, *The Cult of the Nation in France: Inventing Nationalism, 1680-1800* (Cambridge, MA: Harvard University Press, 2001), p. 15.

2. David F. Burg, *A World History of Tax Rebellions: An Encyclopedia of Tax Rebels, Revolts, and Riots from Antiquity to the Present* (New York: Routledge, 2004), p. xvi.

Chapter 3. Jacobins, Emperors, and Kings

1. "Declaration of the Rights of Man: 1789." Avalon Project—Documents in Law, History and Diplomacy. http://avalon.law.yale.edu/18th_century/rightsof.asp

2. Ibid.

3. Lisa Neal, *France: An Illustrated History* (New York: Hippocrene Books, 2001), p. 162.

Chapter 4. The World at War

1. Mike Dash, "Curses! Archduke Franz Ferdinand and His Astounding Death Car." *Smithsonian Magazine*, April 22, 2013. http://blogs.smithsonianmag.com/history/2013/04/curses-archduke-franz-ferdinand-and-his-astounding-death-car/

2. Jonathan Fenby, *The General: Charles de Gaulle and the France He Saved* (New York: Skyhorse, 2012), p. 198.

3. Ibid., p. 139.

Chapter 5. Vive La Différence (Long Live the Difference)

1. Jacques Chirac and Catherine Spencer, *My Life in Politics* (New York: Palgrave Macmillan, 2012), p. 154.

2. Aurélie Filipetti, "Our Ambitions for Cultural Diplomacy in the 21st Century." France in the United States: Embassy of France in Washington. July 15, 2013. http://www.franceintheus.org/spip.php?article4748

FURTHER READING

Books

Gilbert, Adrian. *The French Revolution*. New York: Thomson Learning, 1995.

Gofen, Ethel, and Blandine Pengili Reymann. *France*. 2nd ed. Tarrytown, NY: Benchmark Books, 2003.

Greenblatt, Miriam. *Napoleon Bonaparte and Imperial France*. New York: Cavendish Square Publishing, 2005.

Sonneborn, Liz. *France: Enchantment of the World*. New York: Scholastic, 2013.

Walker, Ida. *France* (Countries of the World). Minneapolis, MN: Essential Library, 2011.

On the Internet

"Napoleon Bonaparte (1769–1821)." BBC History.
http://www.bbc.co.uk/history/historic_figures/bonaparte_napoleon.shtml

"France Timeline." Time for Kids Around the World.
http://www.timeforkids.com/destination/france/history-timeline

Works Consulted

Bell, David Avrom. *The Cult of the Nation in France: Inventing Nationalism, 1680–1800*. Cambridge, MA: Harvard University Press, 2001.

Burg, David F. *A World History of Tax Rebellions: An Encyclopedia of Tax Rebels, Revolts, and Riots from Antiquity to the Present*. New York: Routledge, 2004.

Burnham, Robert, editor-in-chief, The Napoleon Series. http://www.napoleon-series.org/index.html

Chirac, Jacques, and Catherine Spencer. *My Life in Politics*. New York: Palgrave Macmillan, 2012.

Dash, Mike. "Curses! Archduke Franz Ferdinand and His Astounding Death Car." *Smithsonian Magazine*, April 22, 2013.
http://blogs.smithsonianmag.com/history/2013/04/curses-archduke-franz-ferdinand-and-his-astounding-death-car/

"Declaration of the Rights of Man: 1789." Avalon Project—Documents in Law, History and Diplomacy. http://avalon.law.yale.edu/18th_century/rightsof.asp

"English terms the language police want barred from French." The Local – France's News in English, September 4, 2013.
http://www.thelocal.fr/galleries/culture/top-ten--latest-english-words-to-toruble-french-language-police/

Fenby, Jonathan. *The General: Charles de Gaulle and the France He Saved*. New York: Skyhorse, 2012.

FURTHER READING

Filipetti, Aurélie. "Our Ambitions for Cultural Diplomacy in the 21st Century." France in the United States: Embassy of France in Washington. July 15, 2013. http://www.franceintheus.org/spip.php?article4748

Gildea, Robert. *Children of the Revolution: The French, 1799–1914*. Cambridge, MA: Harvard University Press, 2008.

Guérard, Albert Léon. *French Civilization: From Its Origins to the Close of the Middle Ages*. New York: Cooper Square Publishers, 1969.

Hanawalt, Barbara. *The European World, 400–1450*. Oxford, United Kingdom: Oxford University Press, 2005.

Huizinga, Johan. *The Waning of the Middle Ages*. Mineola, NY: Dover, 1999.

Lentze, Georg. "Islamic headscarf debate rekindled in France." BBC News, April 4, 2013. http://www.bbc.co.uk/news/world-europe-21997089

McPhee, Peter. *A Social History of France, 1789–1914*. 2nd ed. New York: Palgrave Macmillan, 2004.

Neal, Lisa. *France: An Illustrated History*. New York: Hippocrene Books, 2001.

Read, Piers Paul. *The Dreyfus Affair: The Scandal that Tore France in Two*. New York: Bloomsbury Press, 2012.

"Roman Sites in France." Historvius: Mapping History. http://www.historvius.com/features/roman-sites-in-france/

Rosenfeld, Sophia A. *Common Sense a Political History*. Cambridge, MA: Harvard University Press, 2011.

Sheffield, Dr. Gary. "The Origins of World War One." BBC History, August 3, 2011. http://www.bbc.co.uk/history/worldwars/wwone/origins_01.shtml

Thompson, J. M. *The French Revolution*. New York: Oxford University Press, 2001.

Timmerman, Kenneth R. *The French Betrayal of America*. New York: Crown Forum, 2004.

Unwin, Brian. *Terrible Exile: The Last Days of Napoleon on St. Helena*. London: I.B. Tauris, 2010.

Wyatt, Caroline. "French headscarf ban opens rifts." BBC, February 11, 2004. http://news.bbc.co.uk/2/hi/3478895.stm

GLOSSARY

abdicated (AB-dih-kay-tuhd)—Gave up one's throne.

bicameral legislature (by-CAAM-uhr-uhl LEG-iss-lay-chur)—A government lawmaking body with two houses, or chambers.

coup (COO)—A sudden, often violent overthrow of the government, usually by the military.

democracy (duh-MAW-cruh-see)—A system of government in which the people elect their leaders.

divine right (duh-VINE RITE)—Belief that a ruler's power comes from God, not man.

extremist (eks-TREE-must)—An individual who refuses to compromise a set of beliefs and demands.

feudalism (FYOO-duhl-izm)—A system in which nobles and lords are given land by the king in exchange for their military support.

guilds (GIHLDS)—Organizations formed by merchants and skilled craftsmen to protect their interests.

guillotine (GHEE-oh-teen)—A device used to behead people, consisting of a heavy blade sliding down between two parallel grooves.

moderate (MAH-duhr-uht)—Person whose beliefs lie between two extremes.

monarchy (MAHN-ar-kee)—A form of government in which a king or emperor rules, usually for life.

politics (PAWL-uh-tiks)—The activities connected with governing a nation.

republic (ree-PUB-lik)—A system of government in which laws are made by elected leaders.

royalist (ROY-uhl-ist)—One who supports a monarchy.

socialist (SOH-shull-ist)—Person who believes that property should be controlled by the state, with profits distributed equally in the form of social welfare.

taxes (TAK-uhz)—Money taken by the government from income, sales, property or other sources and used to pay for programs and facilities.

INDEX

About the Author

Born in Boston, Massachusetts, John Bankston began writing articles while still a teenager. Since then, over 200 of his articles have been published in magazines and newspapers across the country, including travel articles in The Tallahassee Democrat, The Orlando Sentinel, and The Tallahassean. He is the author of over 60 biographies for young adults, including Alexander the Great, scientist Stephen Hawking, author F. Scott Fitzgerald, and actor Jodi Foster.